Above and Beyond 2017

© 2018 What Is God Doing Now

All Rights Reserved.

No part of this book may be reproduced, stored in a retrieval system, or transmitted by any means without the written permission of the author. The views expressed in this book are those of the authors and do not necessarily represent or reflect the views of this publishing company.

Published by Word Therapy Publishing, LLC

February 20, 2018

ISBN-13: 978-0975516355

ISBN-10: 0975516353

Printed in the United States of America all rights reserved under international Copyright laws.

Cover Design by: Toni Henderson-Mayers

Word Therapy Publishing

P.O. Box 939

Hope Mills, NC 28348

www.wordtherapypublishing.com

Above and Beyond 2017

Above and Beyond 2017

Preface

I hope that this book assists you in your everyday decision making and spiritual development in your relationship with God our heavenly father. In memory of my mother Josephine Pasty Bryant who I always will love very dearly now in heaven. To my wife Prophetess Katrina Lee, a dedicated prophetic voice during these end-times. Also, a special thanks to Ms. Bernice Walker-Gardner and Amy McCoy a member who have been a tremendous blessing to me both dedicated to the things of the Lord. Also to one of our members Prophetess D. Tu who never left her post with us and stood in the gap and prays for us.

Above and Beyond 2017

Table of Contents

1. Knowledge vs Revelation Knowledge
2. Demonic Attacks
3. Reconstruction Period
4. 7-year Revival Coming
5. Holy Spirit Led
6. Whole Nations
7. Corruption
8. Years of Acceleration
9. Prophetic Season
10. North Korea
11. A List Of Happenings Now And Beyond

Above and Beyond 2017

Chapter 1

Knowledge vs Revelation Knowledge

I admit throughout the years while visiting many churches, not as a speaker but as a guest, many of those preachers were very good speakers, I don't deny that. Also, many of those leaders were highly respected within the churches they governed. Schools of theology is knowledge about the bible and so forth, and some of those ministers probably went to school, I am sure. A few of them I know personally. My point is just knowing bible stories is not enough. Knowing a lot about the bible can cause a person to become puffed up and full of pride.

Despite the excellent sermons heard and many challenging conversations I engaged in years ago to prove my point, a huge number of church people still have very challenging issues. I had to be honest with myself going to church eventually took a toll on me back in 1988-1989. I decided to take a year off from church (not God) to re-organize my life. During that time God was not the problem or the blame. I realized my life was a mess. The question I had to ask myself was how can I preach to a group of people if they have the same problems I am struggling with? Similar situations to mine happen all the time in ministry and am sure nationally there are churches with excellent preachers which there is no shortage of.

It seems the word "apostle" or "prophet" is on every church door post nowadays. One of my augments is sermons about the bible are preached every week but the question remains does it help the people grow or is it just noise. Noise keeps church people religious and ineffective toward the kingdom of God. What noise am I talking about? How about the loud beating of drums or the loud organ? Many times I barely enjoyed the preaching because of it.

Above and Beyond 2017

Churches should be audited and records should be pulled regarding the source of information provided to its followers. Why not? The church receives a lot of help from the 'federal government' through the 501c3 labeled a non-profit organization. My arugment accurate information from the bible and learning how to apply it correctly is critical to every born-again or believer's spiritual growth. Hosea 4:6

Again, my goal is not to bad mouth the body of Christ, the goal is to cause you as an individual to think outside the box or familiar surroundings and take charge of your own spiritual growth through asking the Lord for revelation knowledge or what I call the most creditable information a person can receive living here on this planet.

Take for example Dr. Fedrick K. Price, he is an excellent teacher in the body of Christ that adds tremendous value and excellence while teaching. Invite him to speak for a few months at any church around the world and guess what you'll get the desired results. 1 Cor 3.7

In the natural it is a fact college educated people have an advantage over people that never went to college in some cases, especially in the market place.

College graduates earn more money is a fact because employers know what they can sometimes bring to the table. Having accurate or revelatory knowledge determines the outcome of many things in this life. Many ministry gifts remain undeveloped due to a lack of revelation knowledge.

The Lord said son over 50% of ministry gifts don't make it! Knowing that humbled me knowing I could easily end up in that same category if I wasn't careful. A lack of revelation knowledge keeps some church people and ministry gifts in an immature state for years. Many are left to fend for themselves even though they faithfully support their local pastor. We need more than bible stories. We need knowledge revealed by the Holy Spirit and applied to our daily lives to be considered an overcomer mature follower of Christ.

Today's call is for men and women in ministry is to provide revealed knowledge by the Holy Spirit which qualifies one to effectively feed God's people. Matthew 16:17

Only God can provide revelatory knowledge to mankind through the Holy Spirit, any other knowledge including "will power" is weak and very limited in its use.

Above and Beyond 2017

(1) As you read the word ask our heavenly father to reveal revelation knowledge to us according to this passage. Ephesians 1:17

(2) That I may know him and the power of his resurrection, and the fellowship of his sufferings, being made conformable unto his death. Philippians 3:10

(3) To know God's will, you must know his ways, and his acts according to (psalm 103:7). You can pray these scriptures over yourself and family, I did and

saw a a big change in my spiritual growth and received more answers to my prayers. Be very specific with what you're asking for.

Chapter 2

Demonic Attacks

I am under heavy demonic attack even as I continue writing this book. What can separate me from the love of God which is in Christ Jesus? Romans 8:31-39

I noticed as I began teaching on the spirit of 'jezebel" and the python spirits brought heavy demonic attacks against me from the spirit realm. Keep in mind that these types of spirits are real and only the anointed power of God can deal with such spirits and defeat them. They are "principalities" spoken of in the book of

Above and Beyond 2017

Ephesians 6:12 and they seek not to be exposed or uncovered. These types of spirits have torn churches apart and heavily exist in the work place or some use the language the marketplace. Witches must work and punch a clock as well and the sad part about it they are also involved in human resources departments in charge of hiring personnel. I admit mot knowing it all remaining humble and always willing to learn new things concerning the Lord.

In the month of March 2017, I can sense a heavy demonic attack on not just me but anybody in the body of Christ standing up for the truth. Regardless of their ministry title or rank. One important point I do want to make of all this we teach sometimes (that statement) that we are personally are fighting these entities and so forth is not the truth. Apostle Paul clearly stated we are "fighting the good fight of faith" 1 Timothy 6:12

These demonic spirits were here before man and are far more intelligent and willing to pull every trick in the book to deceive mankind and destroy planet earth if it had not been for the resurrection of our Lord and savior Jesus Christ.

One of the spiritual gifts "discerning of spirits' is desperately needed in every ministry gift today. One of the major problems we have in the body of Christ today is some of us lacking badly lacking in this gift of the Holy Spirit. I personally believe that's the reason a lot of ministries shy away from deliverance in their ministries knowing within themselves the ability to discern and cast out demons of various types is just not there. A lot of us are too proud to admit it but this is a true statement for the moment that will change shortly. God's reconstruction of the church is underway. You can't fight demons in your own strength especially without the gifts of the Holy Spirit.

For the most part without gifts a person or ministry have no clue in what they are dealing with until after all the damage has already been done. Going forward we need strong deliverance ministries that can cast out devils. Many of God's people are bound and need deliverance from various types of demonic oppression. The good news is I do believe God is raising up a "new breed" or the sons of God with new oil during this reformation period to destroy and root out the devil.

Above and Beyond 2017

(1) Who can cast out devils in the name of Jesus? And these signs shall follow them that believe; In my (name) shall they cast out devils. Mark chapter 16

(2) Jesus was simply saying that in his name believers would have authority over the devil. They will break the power of the devil over their own lives and the lives of their love ones. They would be free from the enemy because they would exercise authority over them.

(3) Notice again Jesus didn't say a word about praying to God or Jesus to do something about devils. Jesus said that believers would do it. Believers will cast out devils. Believers would speak with new tongues. Believers would lay their hands on the sick and they would recover. Be encouraged, we have the power and authority only in the name of Jesus. It belongs to every believer. The Lord shared with me in 2017 that during this re-construction period of the church

there will be a restoral of exercising (authority over devils like we never seen before) with authority just like Jesus did when he was here on planet earth.

Chapter 3

Re-Construction Period

The church is in the process of a "reformation period" were God is cleaning house and right now we desperately need people that can interpret what the spirit of the Lord is saying and inject that message into the hearts and minds of the people. While reading this book one might ask themselves what does a reformation mean? One definition of this is reformation means making changes to something with the intention of setting it back on the right path. Right now, the church appears asleep and is being "awaken" by God to return to the position. There needs to be a place of authority and influence. That position also involves a stance to exercise authority of demonic powers and get immediate results by using the name of Jesus. Acts 3:6

A prior reconstruction period for example under a previous religious revolution that took place in the western church in the 16th century. Its greatest leaders undoubtedly were Martin Luther and Jon Calvin just to mention a few of them. Having far-reaching political, economic, and social effects on the church at that time. This reformation became the (basis) for the founding of (Protestantism) one of three major branches of Christianity. The purpose of re-construction or reformation is restoration and to purge the church of medieval abuses and immoralities and restore true doctrine and practices that the reformers believed conformed with the bible and the new testament model of the church. In 1517 Martin Luther, a "German Augustinian Monk" challenged some portions of roman catholic doctrine and several specific practices.

During this current reformation under way the Lord is shaking church foundations and re-aligning them for his eternal purposes he has for the church. We are in it now and a lot of Christian people who know what is going on are excited. The goal of this book is not to convince the reader about the history of "Martin Luther" but to focus more on the fact that God is once again changing the face of the church to what it should look like. Major changes are in progress God being the master builder. During re-construction of course, it brings a certain amount of resistance. Sometimes people rather stay in the same old rut. Some will turn bitter, speak against it without realizing that God is the one behind the re-construction. For so long the church has been weak, lacking the ability to demonstrate the power of the resurrected Christ the early church in the book of Acts had.

A lot of the information that I am providing in this material is information revealed to me during periods of spending time seeking the face of God and using active listening skills to document what I am being told. We call them Rhemas. A Greek interpretation is defined as a sudden knowing, having knowledge of something you did not have before. Some call it an on time word of the Lord provided by the Holy Spirit.

Some evangelical Christians however think that Rhemas and the Logos are synonymous but they are not. Many charismatic teachers promote the belief that there is a distinct difference between the Rhema and Logos even though both are translated as "word" in English bibles. Some teach the logos is the written word of God which is the truth just a different translation in Greek. Rhemas on the other hand are believed to be special revelations from God and that also has a lot of truth to it. According to most Greek scholars however there is no validity in the argument that New Testament writers made such a clear distinction between them in their writing. Under God's major re-construction period even subjects like this will be cleared up by those given assignments to do so.

Chapter Four

7 Year Revival Coming

According to what the Lord has shown Apostle Isaiah Kadiri, Pastor of (Amfo) of Africa Mission Field Outreach in Nigeria in Africa is that a "7-year revival is coming to America. The apostle stated that this move of the Father is just at the doorstep in the form of a "third great awakening" something the whole church world has been preparing and interceding for is now in route.

Mr. Kadiri saw a mighty spinning wind that broke off into four different directions starting from the "gulf coast into America" a powerful wind of the Holy Spirit traveling part east, some going west and a part going north and the rest going south parts of the world. This powerful wind of the Holy Spirit will clear everything in its pathway according to what he saw. This revival will turn God's people back to him "Saith the Lord". I will refine the bride and then the trumpet will sound. We are in a major preparation for God's end time harvest of souls, and believe me my friend it is harvest time. Mathew 4:19

I believe other prophetic camps around the world including prophets in the

Above and Beyond 2017

United states of America are all hearing God speak to them along these same lines, submitting ourselves one to another regardless of what prophetic camp you belong to. Putting all the pieces of the puzzle together to get a better understanding of what the Lord is doing and saying. Isaiah 28:10

We all have one heavenly father that speaks similar words to his prophets regardless of what prophetic team you're with there is only one Lord. Ephesians 4:4-6

Prophetic Camps or ministries that I am familiar with include prophets from ministries below; even though there are so many more:

1. Kenneth Copeland Ministries
2. Bill Hamon from Christian International Ministries
3. Cindy Jacobs from Generals International
4. James W. Goll from God Encounters Ministries

The Lord has also shown to many credible prophets in the land that this is going to be the best of times and the worst of times all at the same time. Amos 3:7

According to the above passage it states surely the sovereign Lord does nothing without first revealing his plan to his servants the prophets. New international translation According to the above translation it states surely the Lord does nothing unless he reveals his secret counsel to his servants the prophets. New American standard translation

Above are just a few translations of many to provide to the reader a clear picture and better understanding of this passage of material.

Above and Beyond 2017

I embraced a statement once made by prophetic voice (Rick Joyner) from Morningstar Ministries: That we desperately need men and women who can interpret accurately what God is doing and saying in these rapidly changing times we live in. Even today we still need wise men and scribe writers. To keep simple and publish what the Lord is saying to his people around the world.

Although wise men were called the "three Kings" the bible does not say how many there were or that they were kings. They were men of learning and they were certainly men of great learning that is one fact we know according to the bible. (Matthew 2:1-12)

Please keep in mind with every major revival comes opposition in the form of a persecution. Mark 4:17

Trust me a true revival will bring all kinds of opposition. 1 Corinthians 16: 8-9

Only God can call forth a true revival that comes about through true repentance. 2 Chronicles 7:14

Chapter 5

Holy Spirit Led

I remember having a conversation with the Lord on 3/6/17 and it was a two-way conversation and one of the things he mentioned was what his battles with the "body of Christ" were and he stated half of his battle is if he could get his people to be spirit led and the other half of his battle is to get us to believe his word that mean verbatim. Now let me mention God our father is talking about being led by the Holy Spirit. Romans 8:14

Above and Beyond 2017

Immediately after typing this I received revelation knowledge how holy to the highest order the Father is something we could ever explain in a life-time. Listen to me very carefully even in minor details no matter how small he wants to be right there to guide us by his Holy Spirit.

God our Father wants to have an intimate relationship with all his children individually and the word states he has no respecter of persons. (Romans 2:11)

During 911 when the twin towers collapsed in New York the Lord told me he spoke to all his children that day about not

going to work individually as they prepared
work a normal workday. He never intended
for any of his children under covenant to
lose their lives that day when both the Twin
Towers and World Trade Center came
crashing down in New York City.
Regardless of your doomsday prophets and
many conspiracies God protects his own.
Our job is to pay very close attention to the
gentle promptings of the Holy Spirit
including 'restrains". Acts 21: 1-26

Though the Spirit they told Paul not
to go on to Jerusalem. But when our days
there were ended, we departed and went on
our journey; (acts 21: 4-5 rsv modified).

Violation of these restrains given by the Holy Spirit could cost a person there lives. My point Christian people were also warned that day during 911 but some died tragically anyway due to failure to recognize the restraints or gentle promptings of the Holy Spirit not to do something.

My goal in my writings is honesty and being straight-forward with you as you read this material. No matter what your purpose is in life if you're going to be successful in your endeavors listening to God must be your number one priority. The formation and answers to your prayers received from the Lord is the most accurate knowledge one can receive in this life.

God knows the total past, present, and future that's why he is God. This is the only way I can describe what I am saying because spiritual things are not always the easiest to describe. We as a body of Christ also as individuals must do whatever it takes to develop that type of relationship with the Lord. The solution to having a better relationship with the Lord varies from person to person. Some may need to fast more to quiet down the flesh or others may need to pray more or a combination of both.

This material is not designed to blame or find fault but to cherish God's people. This book can only be used as a guide or provide a means of instruction. I cannot stress enough that the most credible information one needs can only be provided directly by the Holy Spirit as we get closer to God. This life of being led by the Holy Spirit is not automatic it requires total submission. The Holy Spirit is actively involved in a surrendered lifestyle. There are three that bear record in heaven the Father, Son, and the Holy Spirit all three are one. 1 John 5:7

Above and Beyond 2017

What I realize if a person is being led by God's spirit they are not under the law and that's were true freedom really is. A religious (demon) has deceived some sincere Christians in the dark from enjoying all that our heavenly father has promised us especially when it comes to being led by the Spirit of God. My goal is not to look anything like other books you may have read, but to be myself and provide you with information it took me years to learn.

Being led by the Lord simple means doing what he tells you to do and nothing more than that. Serious problems arise between us and him when we want to do things our way. Over the years even in ministry some still refuse to let God promote and establish them. Acts 16:9

Below are three things that will make you more aware of these gentle promptings:

1. Keep this book of the law always on your lips, mediate on it day and night so that you may be careful to do everything written in it. Then you will be prosperous and successful. Joshua 1:8
2. Instantly obey the gentle promptings will cause you to

become more aware of his leadings. Romans 8:14

3. Be a doer of the word not just a listener only causes your spirit man to be more sensitive of the leading of God. James 1:22

Chapter 6

Whole Nations

Right around the beginning of the year 2018 as I was laying in bed relaxing the Lord began speaking to me about how he is about to save whole nations. I asked no questions but quickly applied my listening skills to what he was saying. Large numbers of people were saved before in history and trust me the Lord can do it again even in large numbers. There were 3000 on the "Day of Pentecost" who responded to Peter's preaching (Acts 2:41).

When anybody reads the book of Acts and all that happened, it was an amazing story about how a true revival started and finished by the work of the Holy Spirit. Well known Evangelist Billy Graham runs various crusades annually and many souls are won for Christ but now an "awakening" is happening to the body of Christ that will cause crusades like Mr. Grahams to appear to be the norm as we draw closer to Gods perfect will the re-constructed church. The church will no longer be spiritual dead losing its first love as before.

Acts 2:41 states after Peter preached three thousand souls were added unto them. Also, on another occasion according to Acts 4:4. But many who heard the message believed the number of men who believed grew to about five thousand. This did not include the women and children just image the Lord bringing these refreshing times back to his people again is exciting.

Whole nations have turned to God in the past let's consider the Old Testament a minute and take King Jehoshaphat in 2 Chronicles, the kingdoms of Israel faced distress at every turn including from enemies plus distress from within. It came to pass after this also that the children of Moab and the children of Ammon and with them other beside the Ammonites came against Jehoshaphat to battle. Chapter 20 1-4

> (1) And Jehoshaphat feared, and set himself to seek the Lord and proclaimed a fast throughout all Judah.
>
> (2) Then there came some that told Jehoshaphat, saying there cometh a great multitude against thee from beyond the sea on this side Syria and behold they be in Hazazontamar which is Engedi.

(3) And Jehoshaphat feared and set himself to seek the Lord and proclaimed a fast throughout all Judah.

(4) And Judah gathered themselves together to ask help of the Lord even out of all the cities of Judah they came to seek the Lord.

This distress mentioned above caused a corporate fast of the nation to the national address from the leader to call on God for help. Jehoshaphat was not interested in making a television appearance as we see today to just to address the issue, but to call on God first. What happens next was God's spirit fell upon Jahaziel the son of Zechariah verses (14-17) a prophecy went forth to the people.

Ye shall not need to fight in this battle: set yourselves stand ye still and see the salvation of the Lord with you, O Judah and Jerusalem: fear not nor be dismayed; tomorrow go out against them for the Lord will be with you. This was all the King needed to hear Glory to God.

Above and Beyond 2017

1. In this hour we need those in authority to turn to God in times of distress. Including asking God's prophets for assistance.
2. To preach the word beyond the four walls and take the word to the streets.
3. The body of Christ needs to turn form our wicked ways. 2 Chronicles 7:14
4. Pray and thank God for a true revival started by the Holy Spirit not man, even if we need to have a national day of prayer to accomplish it.

Chapter 7

Corruption

In the month of January of 2017 the Lord began dealing with me very strongly about corruption in the United States American government. During that visitation he began sharing with me about how deep this corruption really is and that he is rooting it out during the Donald Trump administration. This corruption consists of voter fraud, taken bribes on the side, plus using campaign funds for one's own personal use, sexual harassment cases plus so much more.

God has already started this process as of late 2017 and will continue until every bit of wickedness has been cleaned out, which may take all or part of Mr. Trumps term done on the Lord's terms not ours. Donald Trump's win to be elected President of the United States was not an accident. The Lord is using him as a trumpet to sound the alarm on corruption that has been in Washington, D.C. for years. He will be a man of courage and will be used to expose corruption during this season says God.

Above and Beyond 2017

His short time in office has been a little rocky which I do believe will straighten itself out as time goes along. Anytime God begins cleaning house things get messy and ugly first. And this is what we're beginning to see in the (news media) reported happenings from Washington D.C...

Over the next four to 8 years the face of government will change with replacements of supreme court judges, senators, republicans and new democrats and so forth. This corruption goes deeper than anyone can imagine with possible arrest coming bringing along with it civil unrest. In this country you're considered innocent until proven guilty. The Lord has had enough of this and people will be removed from office. I suggest that you not be shaken or scared of the things you began to see in the news through television because it is about to go down. I could mention names but it would be inappropriate to do so while writing this book. I will leave the dirty work to be brought out by the news media. One purpose of cleaning things up is that the Lord wants his own people to be in position as well. Proverbs 29.2

Let me mention also that huge division exist between the democrats and republicans and nothing is getting done, and many real issues Americans are concerned about get put on the back burner every day. James 3:16

It is time for real change and of course this change will upset some people. We will see replacements people that are righteous that love God, which makes a major difference with move this country forward (To Make It Great Again).

The news media will try to betray Mr. Trump as a racist which is coming from the demonic realm. But don't worry God has all that under control. If leadership in this country don't repent the Lord will remove some of them even from the face of the earth. The Lord is very serious about his "time clock" and will stay on his schedule no matter what to restore America and reap this last "end-time harvest of souls".

Chapter 8

Years of Acceleration

Acceleration is the name we give to any process where the velocity changes. Since velocity is a speed and a direction, there are only two ways for you to accelerate: change your speed or change your direction—or change both.

If you're not changing your speed and you're not changing your direction, then you simply cannot be accelerating—no matter how fast you're going. So, acceleration occurs when both speed and direction are applied in the same direction. The Lord created and is a master at the laws of physics.

Acceleration is a vector quantity that is defined as the rate at which an object changes its velocity. An object is accelerating if it is changing its velocity not how fast it is going. A person can be moving very fast and still not be accelerating. Acceleration must do with changing how fast an object is moving. If an object is not changing its velocity, then the object is not accelerating. As an object moves, it often undergoes changes in speed.

Above and Beyond 2017

I said all of that to say the Lord is accelerating personal and corporate prophecies worldwide. The years of acceleration has already started and what it took you years to complete will happen in a matter of months if it is God's will for your life. Angels also will play a major role during this acceleration period. Hebrews 1:14

Any unfulfilled prophecies under the Old Testament prophets left will come to pass during this acceleration period. God knows how to take multiply years and compound them all together for his glory. Joel 2:25

Below is a passage of scripture where the Lord used acceleration in someone's life. King Hezekiah's Illness and Recovery

1. Isaiah 38.5
2. 2 kings 20:6

Chapter 9

Prophetic Season

The Lord said to me on 1/24/18, Son, this is a very prophetic season as I laid in bed applying my active listening skills. During this re-construction period keep in mind the foundation of the church is built on the "foundation" of the apostles and prophets, with Christ Jesus himself as chief cornerstone. Ephesians 2:20

Whenever there was a major move orchestrated by God he always used prophets to speak the result into the earthly realm before it happened. This has always been God's way of doing things and this gives a nation or individuals including the "body of Christ" a chance to prepare themselves first and that's a fair God say amen! And since the Lord is rebuilding the church he said to me son am calling for my true prophets to (sound the alarm) judgment is coming.

Judgement is coming upon this world's "Babylonian System" a system with mankind trying to meet all his needs without God. Please note that even though this is a very prophetic season it also is a time of judgement for the world and the covers of wickedness will be pulled off many individuals including clergy/rapper-people in the music industry/ national sports figures/ politicians along with movie directors and actors.

I mentioned in a previous chapter that when God begins some major construction projects things get real messy at first because you must first tear things down and start rebuilding. I believe God will remove some people through physical death including clergy if need be to accomplish his purposes, pursues, and plans. Hebrews 10:31

God is very serious about what he is trying to accomplish in this season and is calling for leaders of churches to pass the torch. God's investment is in a company of prophets not a single individual to stand up and declare "Thus Saith the Lord". The adjustments and realignments are already underway and you will either shape up or ship out to what God is doing. God during re-construction is using prophets to uproot and tear down first then re-build and plant. Jeremiah 1:10

A New Testament prophet consists of more than just prophesying it involves speaking on behalf of God. A major role of the prophet office is to be a (forerunner).

Above and Beyond 2017

During this very prophetic season, it will be a company of forerunners probably thousands coming in advance to prophesy the arrival of things the Lord is already doing now and beyond. God is the same his method and ways of during things will not change. Hebrews 13:8

{On 12/16/17 the Lord gave me these words concerning the prophets}.

I will begin to speak to my prophets with such clarity it will seem unprecedented. Like I said in my word. I will do nothing except I first reveal it first to my servants the prophets. Some will say within themselves he could not have known this without the help of the Lord!

Prophetic flow- And it is coming out like water through a faucet. I am beginning to stir up my people for what am about to do in this earth realm. This prophetic flow is branching off into two different directions the seer's realm and the other prophetic realm. (Saith the Lord)

Some refer to this as prophetic streams that I will have to cover in a future book. Prophets will continue to prepare the way for all God wants to accomplish in this prophetic season now and beyond.

Chapter 10

North Korea

Kim Jong-un or Kim Jong Un is the Chairman of the Workers' Party of Korea and supreme leader of North Korea since 2011. Kim is the second child of Kim Jong-il and Ko Yong-hui. The Lord began dealing with me regarding this family on 01/29/18 in a strong way. This family has a history of pure evil where even family members have been executed. One his uncle Jang Song-thaek for reports of alleged "treachery" in December of 2013 and the allegations Mr. Jong-un ordered the assassination of his half-brother, Kim Jong-nam in Malaysia in February 2017.

The Lord began sharing with me how this family feels no obligation or commitment towards him at all. That it is a dictatorship where he has sole control over all the people there in North Korea. Over the years the outcry has been for Jung Un to stop his ballistic missile testing. Outrage from the international community including Japan have called on him to disarm. He continues his madness and in February of 2017, North Korea launched what is described as a long-range ballistic missile and then they launched its Hwasong-15 missile, which reached a height of approximately 2,800 miles above ground, before splashing down off the coast of Japan.

At that point North Korea finally finalized and completed its nuclear weapons program, now capable of reaching any location on the planet with a strike. Is he capable of starting "world war three" and the answer to this question is probably yes? What is holding this tragic event from occurring is the prayers of the righteous.
James 5:16

Above and Beyond 2017

I sense in my human spirit that prayer groups all over the country are praying to hold this back possibly for a future time in history. The only one that can hold this event from happening is God himself. 2 Chronicles 7:14

Keep in mind we are still living in very uncertain and dangerous times as well. When the 45th president "Donald John Trump was elected a shift took place after he made commits to Israel to back and stand by them. Mr. Trump is a trumpet the Lord is using to clean up Washington including Wall Street. Even-though Satan wants war for America God says no am not finished with it. The Lord still has a plan for America and will finish the job and make "America Great Again". If the leader of North Korea "Kim Jong-Un" gets in the way of God's plans he will either be assassinated from his own political leaders within or the Lord will remove him from the face of the earth. Far as the Russians are concerned the leader "Vladimir Putin" at some point will be replaced with someone more wicked than himself. If they did tamper with this last election, it all will come out at some point by the news media. China and their president "Xi Jinping" still seem in a state of confusion from all Kim Jong-Un's determination to complete its nuclear program to complete and it created a strained-diplomatic relationship for so time to come.

In my closing it all will play out with the nations just like the Lord said it would now and in the future. Isaiah 55:11

Chapter 11

A List Of Happenings Now And Beyond

1. Broken relationships will be restored a mending back together.
2. Suddenly or unexpected events will happen suddenly for your good. Acts 2:2
3. Major changes coming to the United States under Donald Trump's administration.
4. Juvenile crime will rise along with an increase in school shootings.

5. God's judgement on the Babylonian system man uses to meet his own needs.
6. Corrupt people in positions of power will be exposed including politicians, movie directors, those in sports, including preachers and some in authority will be removed be God.
7. The world will get darker with increased terror.
8. The spirit of perversion is running rapid through the land of America along with increased moral decline.
9. New heavenly assignments handed out by God to man.

10. Increase in angelic activity and visitations on planet earth.
11. America will be great again including economically.
12. Increased discussion to overturn "Roe v Wade.
13. Times of transition.
14. New beginnings.
15. Years of acceleration.
16. Years of sudden breakthroughs.
17. Years of release
18. God is "awakening" his people out of a deep sleep.
19. Reformation years for the church.

20. Times of fabulous "outpourings" by the Holy Spirit upon the church.
21. A company of prophets are sounding an alarm calling the people of God back to holiness.
22. Separation of God's people from the world. 2 Chronicles 7:14
23. Times of fulfillment of all biblical prophecy.
24. Restoral of the "Ascension Gifts" in power on a new breed rising.
25. God is dealing very strongly with current leaders in place to "pass the torch" and if they refuse he may

remove them from the face of the earth.

26. President Donald Trump has been placed in Washington by God and will be used as a triumphant voice to expose corruption including wall street.

27. Possible arrest of head leaders in the FBI plus a more intensive investigation into Hilary Clintons scams and email scandal with indictments ahead.

28. Restoral of power to "cast out devils" like we have never seen before.

29. Great harvest of souls being won.

www.wordtherapypublishing.com

"A Message That Heals"

www.ingramcontent.com/pod-product-compliance
Lightning Source LLC
Chambersburg PA
CBHW060214050426
42446CB00013B/3072